THOSE WHO BULLY AND THOSE WHO ARE BULLIED

A GUIDE FOR CREATING HEROES IN THE CLASSROOM

THE ORP LIBRARY

WRITTEN BY
KRISTIN WESTBERG

BASED ON THE BOOK
CLASSROOM HEROES BY
JEFF KRUKAR, PH.D.
PAMELA DeLOATCH
WITH
JAMES G. BALESTRIERI

Copyright © 2014

All rights reserved. Except as permitted under the
U.S. Copyright Act of 1976, no part of this publication may be
reproduced, distributed, or transmitted in any form or by any
means, or stored in a database or retrieval system, without
the prior written permission of the publisher.

WRITERS OF THE ROUND TABLE PRESS
PO BOX 511
HIGHLAND PARK, IL 60035

Publisher	COREY MICHAEL BLAKE
Workbook Content Writer	KRISTIN WESTBERG
Writing Assistance	LEEANN SANDERS
Post Production	SUNNY DIMARTINO
Director of Operations	KRISTIN WESTBERG
Facts Keeper	MIKE WINICOUR
Cover Design	ADAPTED FROM DESIGN BY ANALEE PAZ
Interior Design and Layout	SUNNY DIMARTINO
Proofreading	RITA HESS
Illustrations	NATHAN LUETH, SHANE CLESTER, SUNNY DIMARTINO

Printed in the United States of America

First Edition: August 2014
10 9 8 7 6 5 4 3 2 1

Library of Congress Cataloging-in-Publication Data
Westberg, Kristin
Those who bully and those who are bullied / Kristin Westberg with
Leeann Sanders.—1st ed. p. cm.
Print ISBN: 978-1-939418-56-2
Library of Congress Control Number: 2014942603

RTC Publishing is an imprint of Writers of the Round Table, Inc.
Writers of the Round Table Press and the RTC Publishing logo
are trademarks of Writers of the Round Table, Inc.

CONTENTS

LESSON 1: WHAT IS BULLYING? · 1

LESSON 2: SOCIAL OR RELATIONAL? · 2

LESSON 3: CAN YOU SPOT A BULLY? · 5

LESSON 4: IS THIS BULLYING? · 8

LESSON 5: THE BULLYING TRIANGLE · 11

LESSON 6: BULLYING IMPACTS EVERYONE · 14

LESSON 7: WHY DO PEOPLE BULLY? · 18

LESSON 8: WHAT'S THE BIG DEAL? SIDE EFFECTS OF BULLYING · 20

LESSON 9: NAVIGATING THE CHALLENGES OF BULLYING · 22

LESSON 10: CONFLICT · 26

LESSON 11: MISSION: BULLY-PROOFING MYSELF · 28

LESSON 12: BREATHE EASY · 30

LESSON 13: WHO I AM · 32

LESSON 14: POSITIVE SELF-TALK · 33

LESSON 15: STICKS AND STONES CAN BREAK MY BONES . . . AND WORDS CAN REALLY HURT ME! · 35

LESSON 16: BE AN UPSTANDER · 38

LESSON 17: SHOWING COMPASSION & UNDERSTANDING FOR THE BULLY, TOO · 40

LESSON 18: THE COMMUNITY CHALLENGE · 42

LESSON 19: WE CAN ALL BE HEROES · 44

LESSON 20: WE ARE HOW WE TREAT EACH OTHER AND NOTHING MORE · 46

RESOURCES · 47

BIOGRAPHIES · 49

ABOUT THESE LESSONS

These lessons were designed so that they can be completed individually, in a classroom, or in a group setting. They are meant to generate discussion around the topic of bullying, help students develop a vocabulary that describes their thoughts, feelings, and what they see happening around them. An effort was made in these lessons to avoid labeling individuals as *bullies* or *victims*. Instead, certain scenarios will refer to these individuals as *students who are bullied*, and *students who bully others*. These lessons can be used in order or you can skip to a lesson to address a specific need or concern your students have.

NOTES FOR FACILITATORS

Specific notes will be provided in a Facilitator's Guide that gives tips or suggestions for how to implement a lesson or tailor the lessons for students with special needs. You know your students best. This guide takes your students on a journey through bullying challenges, but it is up to you to help them navigate the lessons based on your needs and current situations that your students might be experiencing. The Facilitator's Guide for this workbook is provided free and is available online at *www.orp.com/library*.

Overall Goals of the Guide

1. Initiate open dialogue about bullying: Use a variety of activities designed to create a dialogue and understanding of the topic that can be used in the classroom, in small groups, in therapy sessions, or even at the dinner table.

2. Engage participants in identifying and defining bullying and the effects of bullying on every individual: including the student who is bullying others, the student who is being bullied, and the bystanders/potential heroes.

3. Assist students in identifying specific bullying challenges that occur in school, home, community, and online and understanding how to navigate those challenges.

4. Develop social skills and problem-solving skills for increased confidence in specific situations, effective responses, providing tools for students to emotionally self-regulate and respond appropriately when confronted with bullying situations.

5. Encourage the development of self-esteem through a strengths-based approach, while also acknowledging areas for improvement.

6. Create an awareness and understanding that it is also right to care for the student who is bullying *without accepting the bullying behavior.*

7. Foster development of peer relationships and interpersonal respect to ensure a supportive and compassionate school community that does not accept bullying behaviors.

LESSON 1
WHAT IS BULLYING?

What is bullying? Circle the words that best describe what bullying means to you. You can add other terms to the word cloud if others come to mind.

<pre>
                                  tolerate
         repeated   compassion   bystander
                                bullied   stereotype
   hurt   support   pain   love   power
                                                 empathy   bully
           abuse   bullying
   ally   trust   humiliate   attack
          tease   fair   stand
                       unwanted
       taunt   harass
              imbalance   target   anger
                                                              kindness
     responsibility   sympathy   cyberbullying
</pre>

Bullying is defined as "**unwanted** and **intentional** aggressive behavior among school-aged children that involves a real or perceived **power imbalance**. The behavior is **repeated**, or has the potential to be repeated, over time." (Stopbullying.gov)

Translation:

Unwanted: Students who are bullied are hurt or harmed physically or emotionally, and it occurs against their will. Intentional: Bullying is not accidental. The person intends to harm someone else. Power Imbalance: The person doing the bullying is perceived as having more physical or interpersonal power or influence. Repeated: The bullying is frequent.

DID YOU KNOW?

- Bullying affects nearly one in three students in grades 6–10
- 83% of girls and 79% of boys report experiencing bullying or harassment
- Approximately 160,000 students skip school each day because of bullying
- Students with disabilities are two to three times more likely to experience bullying than their nondisabled peers

ACTIVITY: JOURNAL RESPONSE

Do you think bullying is a problem? Why or why not?

_____
_____
_____
_____
_____

LESSON 2
SOCIAL OR RELATIONAL?

Bullying can take on several different forms: verbal, physical, social, and cyberbullying. Read the examples below and add your own examples based on what you think or know.

VERBAL

| Teasing | Calling someone names | Taunting |
| Threatening | Using hurtful or embarrassing words | Other: _____ |

Draw a cartoon of verbal bullying:

PHYSICAL

Hitting	Tripping	Spitting
Kicking	Taking or hiding others' personal property	Other: _____
Pushing		

Draw a cartoon of physical bullying:

SOCIAL

Embarrassing someone

Excluding a child on purpose

Spreading rumors

Telling others not to be friends with that child

Other: _____

Draw a cartoon of social bullying:

CYBERBULLYING

Sending hurtful or threatening text messages

Posting rumors online

Sending hate emails

Other: _____

Draw a cartoon of cyberbullying:

ACTIVITY: PUT YOURSELF IN ANOTHER'S SHOES

This activity can be done with a partner or alone.

1. Discuss, draw, or write what you think the student who is being bullied thinks and feels in one of the situations mentioned on the previous pages.

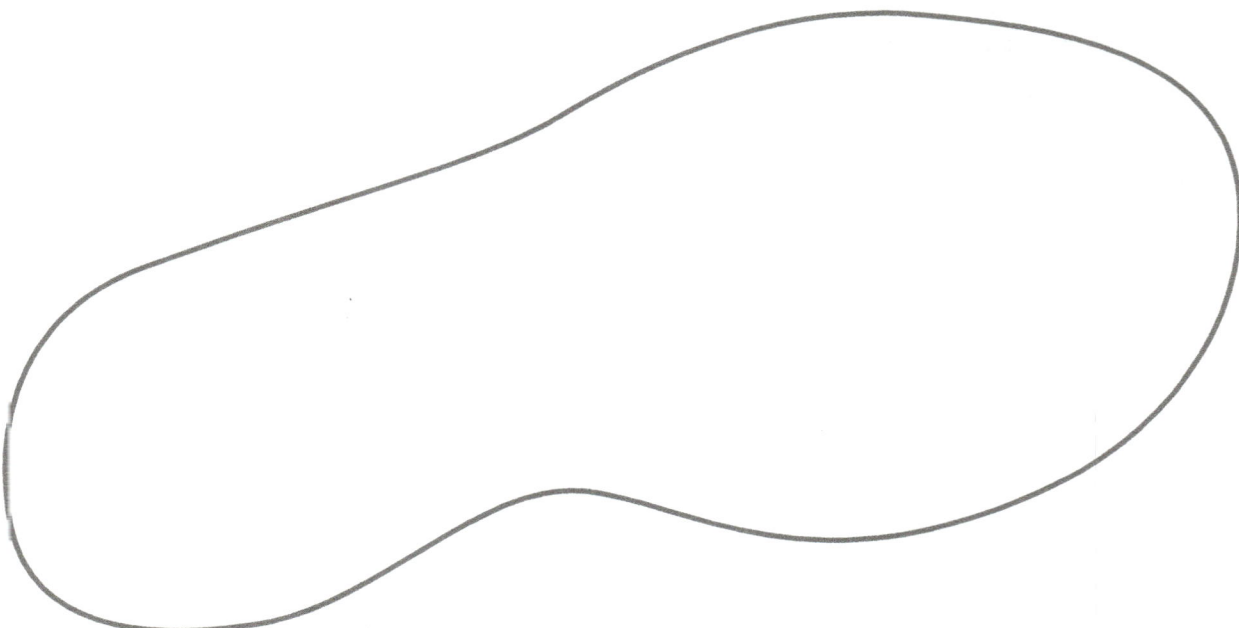

2. Draw what you would think and feel if you were watching any of these bullying situations happen to someone.

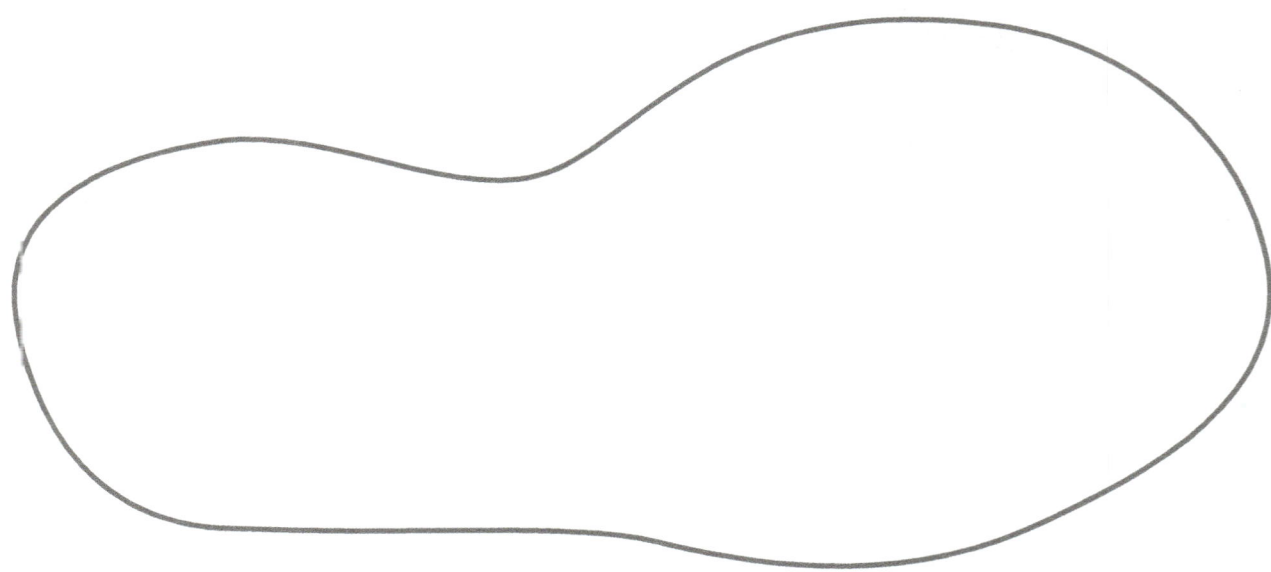

LESSON 3
CAN YOU SPOT A BULLY?

Use the drawing below to help you describe students who bully others.

Anybody can be a bully. Some are popular and have lots of friends. Others are disliked by almost everyone and seem to not have any friends. Bullies **cannot** be recognized by what they look like. They are recognized by their actions, and what they say or do.

One thing that all bullies have in common is their desire for power, control, and influence with little concern for the feelings of others. They sometimes struggle with empathy, which is the ability to understand and relate to how another person is feeling. Often, people who bully have been hurt emotionally themselves in the past.

ARE YOU A BULLY?

Could you be a bully? Maybe you aren't all of the time. But even the nicest of people can bully others in certain situations. In fact, most of us will bully someone else at some point in our lives.

Have you often laughed when someone gets hurt or embarrassed?	☐ Yes ☐ No
Do you enjoy making jokes about people based on their race, culture, or preferences?	☐ Yes ☐ No
Have you forced someone to do something he or she did not want to do?	☐ Yes ☐ No
Do you stand by and watch as someone else is being bullied?	☐ Yes ☐ No
Have you sent mean, nasty, embarrassing, or threatening texts or emails?	☐ Yes ☐ No

If you answered **yes** to any of these questions, you may have engaged in bullying behavior.

ACTIVITY: WRITE A LETTER

Think about a time when you might have been mean to someone or witnessed another student being bullied and did not do anything to stop it. Write a letter to this student sharing what you think and feel and what you have learned about your own behavior. You may use the sample template provided or write your own letter. You do not need to use any names or identify the person: The key to this activity is that you are reflecting on your thoughts, feelings, and behavior—as well as the other person's—and sharing that you care.

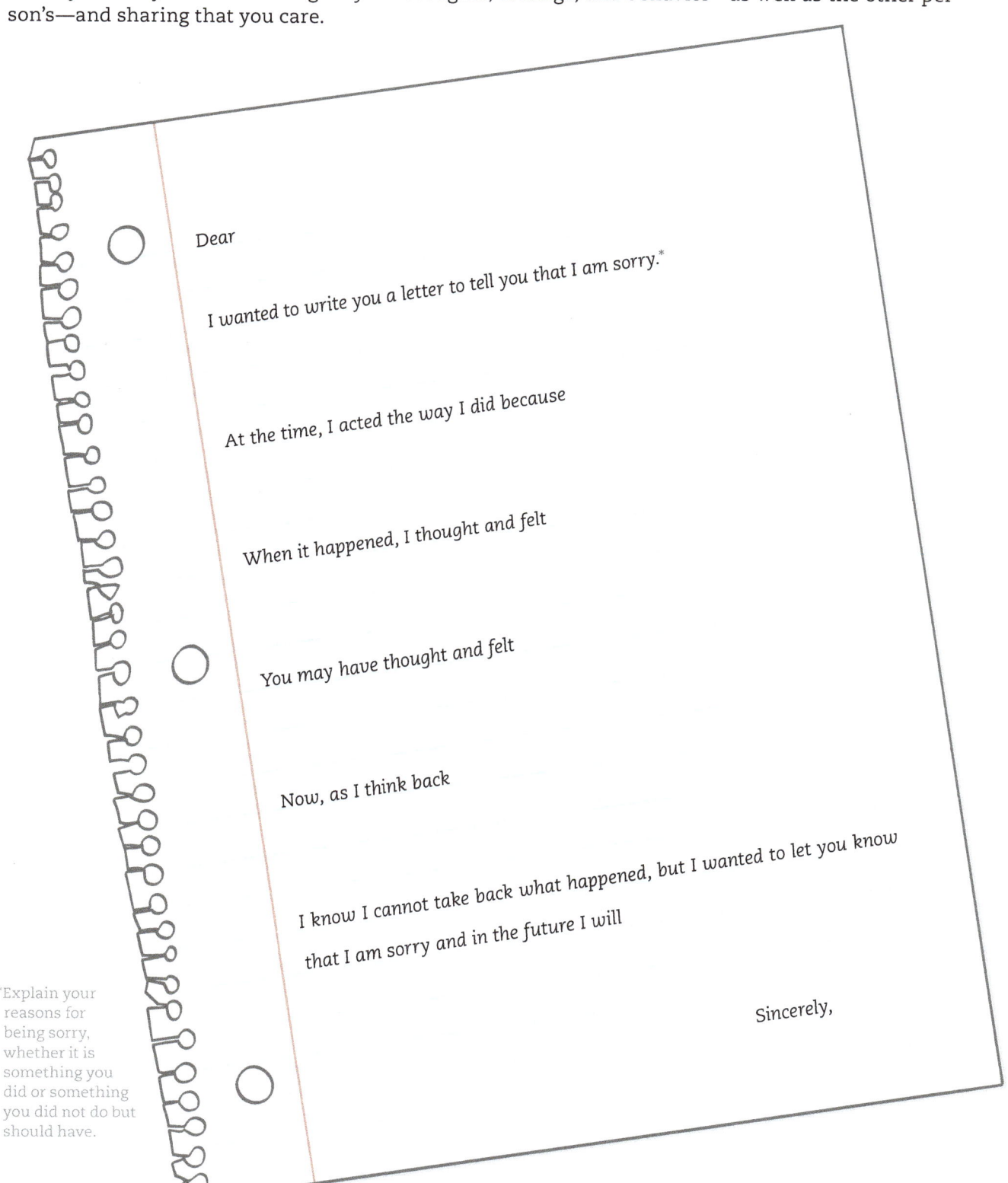

Dear

I wanted to write you a letter to tell you that I am sorry.*

At the time, I acted the way I did because

When it happened, I thought and felt

You may have thought and felt

Now, as I think back

I know I cannot take back what happened, but I wanted to let you know that I am sorry and in the future I will

Sincerely,

*Explain your reasons for being sorry, whether it is something you did or something you did not do but should have.

LESSON 4
IS THIS BULLYING?

For a behavior to be considered bullying, it must meet these 3 requirements:

The action or behavior is **unwanted** by the person experiencing the bullying. A **power imbalance** exists, making it difficult for the person to defend himself or herself from the other person. The action is **repeated**. It happens frequently.

Sometimes we all have experiences that hurt our feelings, are embarrassing, or make us angry. That doesn't necessarily mean that you have been bullied.

Examples:

Not being liked by someone

Not being invited to a birthday party

Someone accidentally hits you with a ball at recess

You get into an argument with a classmate

ACTIVITY: YOU DECIDE!

Look at each of the following scenes. Decide if this is bullying or not, and explain why.

Sample 1

Bullying? Why? Why not?

_____

_____

_____

_____

Sample 2

Bullying? Why? Why not?

_____
_____
_____
_____

Sample 3

Bullying? Why? Why not?

_____
_____
_____
_____

Not everything is bullying. Sometimes people can be embarrassed, have their feelings hurt, or experience another person being rude to them. It's important to recognize the difference, so when you are experiencing bullying (or even bullying someone else), you can help stop the behavior!

ACTIVITY: WHAT IS THIS, THEN?

Mark each behavior below as bullying, embarrassing, or rude. Be prepared to discuss your answers.

B = Bullying   E = Embarrassing   R = Rude

_____ Tara was picked last for a team at recess.

_____ Joe rolled his eyes when Leah raised her hand to answer the question.

_____ Sasha makes sure that Krista has to sit alone at lunch each day.

_____ Todd laughs at people when they trip and fall.

_____ John called Terry a loser after he missed a basket in P.E. class.

_____ Cara gets the entire class to ignore Shelly when she walks into the room each morning.

_____ Mark posted embarrassing pictures of a classmate online and shared them with all of his friends.

_____ Erica sends emails to a classmate every day telling her "No one likes you. You shouldn't even come to school anymore."

_____ A group of students will not make room for someone else to join a full lunch table in the cafeteria.

_____ Ted forces Jacob to eat a live bug or else he will punch him in the face

_____ Jose is threatened by another student if he doesn't give him money.

_____ Tom trips a classmate when she walks by.

_____ Sam mumbles "DORK" under his breath every time Leo walks by.

_____ Adam invites everyone in the class to his birthday party except Shawn.

LESSON 5
THE BULLYING TRIANGLE

Nearly 1 in 5 students will experience bullying in an average classroom. The rest of the students, known as bystanders, are also affected by bullying. When it comes to bullying, everyone is involved.

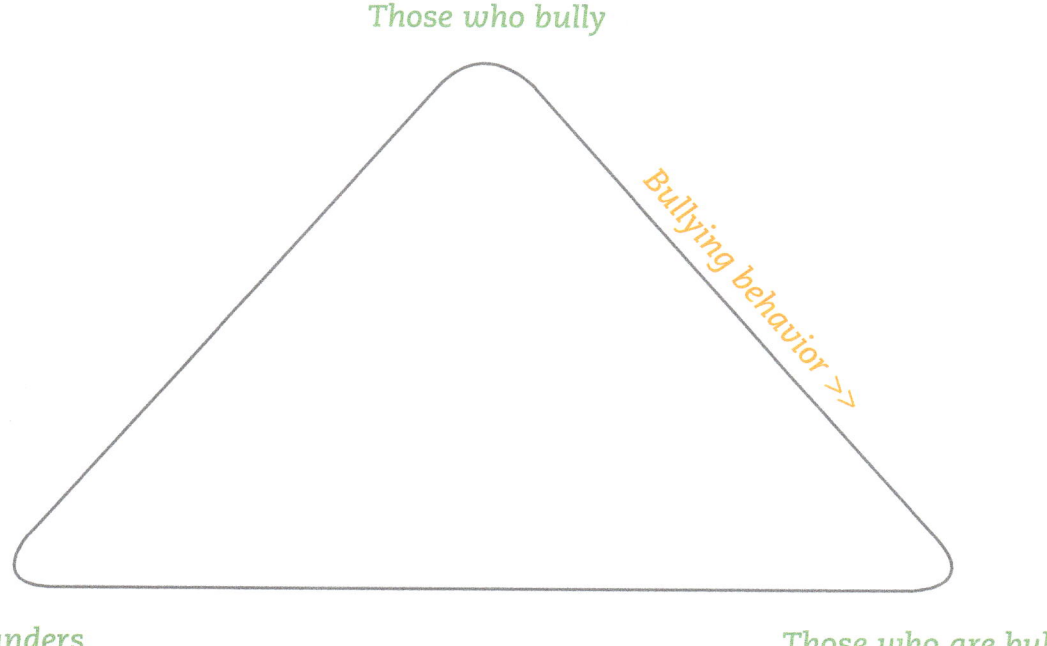

ACTIVITY

Draw a line from each role to its correct description.

1. Those who bully

2. Those who are bullied

3. The bystanders

a. The person who is the target of the bullying behavior

b. The people who are watching the bullying behavior happen to someone else

c. The person who is exhibiting the bullying behavior toward the victim

DISCUSSION ACTIVITY

This activity is best done with a small group of students. Each group should receive a copy of each scenario and its consequence or effect. One student from the group will read the scenario out loud, and the group will decide which effect most matches that situation.

THE BULLYING SCENARIO

I always want to buy snacks after school, so I threaten Adam that if he doesn't buy me something, I won't hang out with him anymore.

THE BULLYING SCENARIO

Every time Jill makes a mistake in class, I laugh and make fun of her.

THE BULLYING SCENARIO

I ignore Tom every day at recess and won't let him play with us. I tell all of my friends to ignore him, too.

THE BULLYING EFFECT

The teacher called my parents because I was bullying another student. I got grounded, and Mom says I was raised better than that. How do I stop?

THE BULLYING EFFECT

Kids are only nice to me because they are afraid of me. I don't have any real friends. Will they find out how sad I really feel?

THE BULLYING EFFECT

Kids think I'm mean. Nobody came to my birthday party. Am I mean for real?

THE BULLIED SCENARIO

I hate going to recess. No one will play with me. They smile and laugh when I ask to play.

THE BULLIED SCENARIO

When the teacher is not looking, Alex flicks me in the back of the head and pokes me in the back. Then he acts like I'm crazy and nothing is happening when I get upset.

THE BULLIED SCENARIO

I was so excited when my grandparents bought me a new cell phone. I gave my number to my friends, but now I'm receiving mean text messages each day from other kids in the 6th grade who found out my phone number.

THE BULLIED EFFECT

I feel so sad and lonely. Some days I don't even want to go to school. Why doesn't anyone like me?

THE BULLIED EFFECT

I'm always nervous and worried at school. I never know if someone is going to hurt me. Why are they always messing with me?

THE BULLIED EFFECT

It's hard to concentrate in school. My grades are dropping, and my teacher has noticed and called my parents. Why are they so mean to me? What did I do?

THE BYSTANDER SCENARIO

Yesterday, in the cafeteria line, Josh kept shoving Trevor into the wall. The teacher did not see him doing it.

THE BYSTANDER SCENARIO

Kelly ignores the new girl in our class and never lets her play with us at recess. She is making fun of her clothes and hair behind her back.

THE BYSTANDER SCENARIO

Andy makes fun of kids in the class and plays mean jokes on others to get people to laugh. It's not funny to me.

THE BYSTANDER EFFECT

I'm afraid to speak up and say anything. Plus, Josh is bigger than me. What if I get bullied too? I don't feel safe in my own school.

THE BYSTANDER EFFECT

It's really difficult to focus and learn when I see others being hurt. but what can I do?

THE BYSTANDER EFFECT

I feel so upset, and I don't know how to help. Should I do something?

LESSON 6
BULLYING IMPACTS EVERYONE

In this activity, you will explore the effects that bullying can have on all the people in the bullying triangle. This is a silent activity.

Read each "big question" and write your thoughts about the topic. Draw lines to connect your thoughts and comments to others. Feel free to respond in writing to others' questions and comments.

BIG QUESTIONS

1. What are the effects of bullying on the person who is being bullied?

2. What are the effects of bullying on the person who is doing the bullying?

3. How does bullying affect the bystanders?

Follow-Up Discussion Questions

In what ways do you see how bullying can have negative effects on all people in the triangle?

_____
_____
_____
_____
_____
_____
_____
_____

How does bullying hurt everyone? Explain.

_____
_____
_____
_____
_____
_____
_____
_____

BIG QUESTION #1

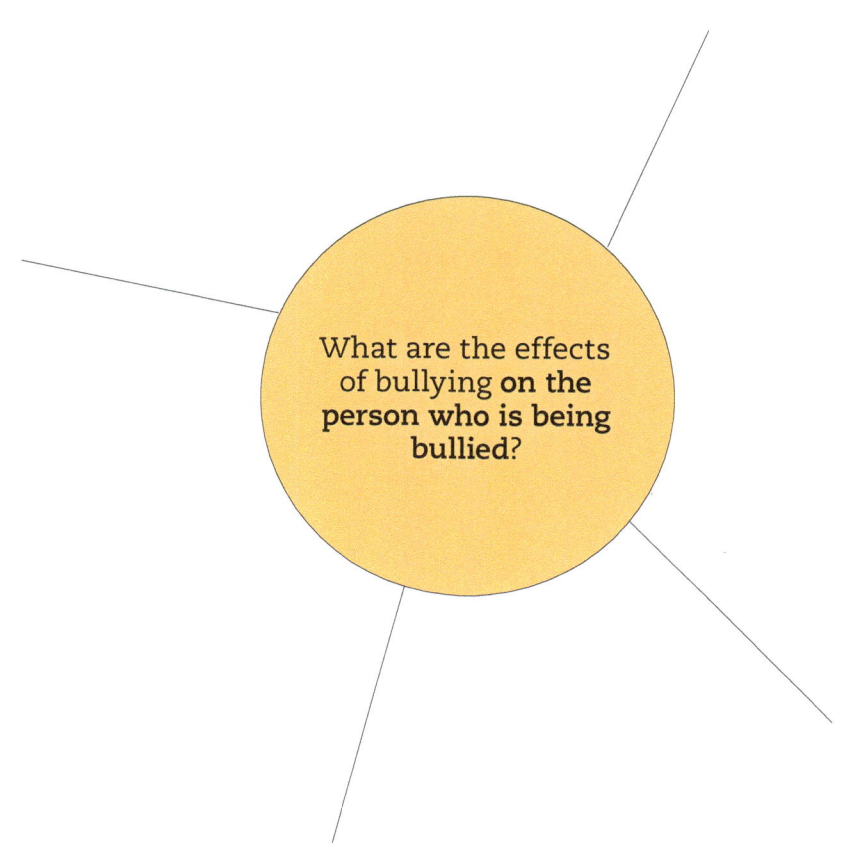

BIG QUESTION #2

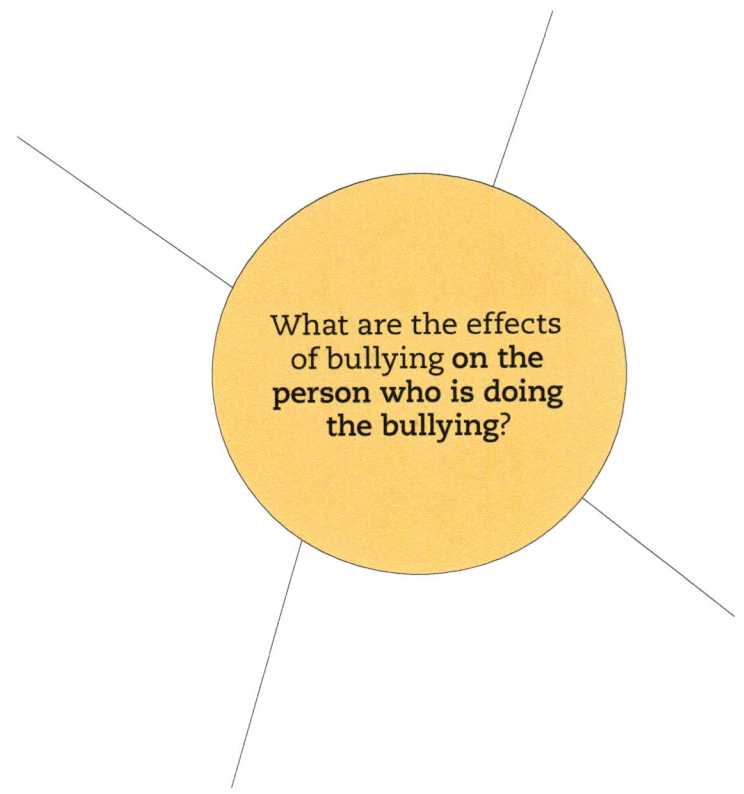

What are the effects of bullying **on the person who is doing the bullying?**

BIG QUESTION #3

How does bullying affect the **bystanders**?

LESSON 7
WHY DO PEOPLE BULLY?

People who bully may be victims of pain and hurt.

In order to feel better about themselves, they might try to use their own power to control a situation. Those who are bullying may want interaction, attention, connection, support, and understanding, even though they might not be able to express those needs in a socially appropriate way. They often have poor social skills.

WHY MIGHT PEOPLE BULLY OTHERS?

Find *some* of the reasons that people might bully or hurt others by completing the word search below.

P	V	I	N	F	Q	M	W	R	B	T	J	D	P	G	U
O	T	S	E	L	S	Y	O	N	O	K	P	Y	O	Q	X
W	M	L	O	Z	C	H	R	T	F	O	I	O	W	B	P
E	D	E	M	B	A	R	R	A	S	S	E	D	E	H	T
R	E	T	P	Y	R	F	I	M	N	L	Y	W	R	S	H
L	S	N	E	S	E	L	E	Y	O	G	K	N	I	D	U
E	U	J	V	M	D	D	D	R	S	D	R	K	M	B	R
S	F	O	S	W	I	U	T	G	U	L	J	Y	F	L	T
S	N	K	T	A	L	N	B	Q	O	G	A	J	D	E	Y
P	O	O	R	S	O	C	I	A	L	S	K	I	L	L	S
G	C	F	E	C	S	G	W	O	A	J	O	W	P	Z	I
D	A	Q	N	R	T	M	Y	L	E	N	O	L	H	B	G
I	L	K	M	E	A	N	U	Y	J	L	T	V	S	A	D

afraid	control	jealous	poor social skills	sad
angry	embarrassed	lonely	power	scared
confused	hurt	mean	powerless	worried

On Your Own:

What are some other reasons why you think people might bully or hurt others? Create your own word search puzzle in the space below. Trade puzzles with a classmate and discuss the reasons you chose the words to include in your own puzzle.

LESSON 8
WHAT'S THE BIG DEAL? SIDE EFFECTS OF BULLYING

So, why is bullying a big deal? Because bullying affects everyone: It affects those who are being bullied, those who are doing the bullying, and those who witness the bullying happening around them. It affects everyone in different ways.

People who experience bullying often feel:

afraid	hopeless	stressed	confused	rejected
unsafe	alone	ashamed	depressed	guilty

Bullying can have many side effects on those who are bullied:

- stress
- depression
- reduced ability to concentrate
- loss of confidence and self-esteem
- problems sleeping – nightmares, bedwetting, unable to sleep
- stomach problems
- panic attacks
- anxiety about going to school
- poor or deteriorating performance in school
- lack of appetite
- lack motivation and energy
- feelings of worthlessness

Even if you are not the one being bullied, witnessing others being hurt can also cause you to experience some of these feelings.

ACTIVITY: HAIKUS

Haiku poetry is a short piece of imaginative writing, usually of a personal nature, that is laid out in three lines: the first line has five syllables, the second line has seven syllables, and the third line again has five syllables. Haikus are usually written about nature or to capture a feeling, mood, or moment.

Write at least one haiku poem about your thoughts and feelings on bullying and the effects of bullying.

Sample haiku (describing the feelings of a person who was bullied):

He cowers in fear
But does not tell anyone
Silently he cries

Write your poem here:

_____

_____

_____

WHAT DO THESE FEELINGS LOOK LIKE?

Create a collage from pictures you find in magazines or newspapers to represent the various feelings and effects that bullying has on people who are bullied and those who witness it. Cut out images and pieces of pictures or draw your own images to help others understand what people who are bullied might feel or experience.

LESSON 9
NAVIGATING THE CHALLENGES OF BULLYING

Where does bullying happen? List the different places you might witness bullying behaviors. (Examples: school locker room, lunch room, playground, etc.)

Bullying Can Happen Anywhere!

If you are being bullied, here are some DOs and DON'Ts!

DOs:

1. DO get away from a situation that feels unsafe.
2. DO tell an adult or someone you can trust what is happening.
3. DO avoid putting yourself in a situation where you are alone with the person who is bullying you.
4. DO stand up for yourself: Be assertive and tell the person bullying you to leave you alone.
5. DO remind yourself that you ARE important and strong, and surround yourself with people who care about you.

DON'Ts:

1. DON'T get aggressive and try to fight.
2. DON'T cry in front of the person bullying you if you can help it.
3. DON'T threaten the person and call him names back.
4. DON'T be passive and ignore the bullying and hope it stops.
5. DON'T believe what the person who is bullying you says about you.

If you witness OTHERS being bullied, here are some things you CAN do:

DOs:

1. DO speak up for the person being bullied.
2. DO let the person being bullied know that he or she isn't alone and has your support: Be kind!
3. DO talk to someone you trust and let him or her know what is happening.
4. DO let the person who is bullying know that you don't agree with what he or she is doing.

ACTIVITY: LETTERS TO THE SCHOOL EDITOR

You can answer these Letters to the School Editor with a partner or on your own. Use some of the strategies we have discussed or come up with your own. In the letters, first tell them what you think they might be thinking or feeling (to practice empathy), and then give them some ideas that might help.

Letter 1

Dear School Editor,

There is a kid in my class that is really mean. He is always making fun of others and laughing at them if they get an answer wrong or are trying to read out loud. He steals other kids' lunches, and they're afraid not to give him what he wants. In fact, many kids are afraid of him. The worst part is, he does all of these things when teachers aren't looking, and he never gets caught. While he doesn't really pick on me, he isn't nice to others and wouldn't let my friend play with us during recess. It really hurt her feelings, and I didn't know what to do. I'm afraid if I say something to him, I'll end up being hurt by him, too. I feel so bad for what is happening to these other kids, but I'm not sure how to help them. What should I do?

Signed,

Confused in My Homeroom

_____
_____
_____
_____
_____
_____
_____
_____
_____
_____

Letter 2

Dear School Editor,

I hate coming to school every day. There's a kid in my class who is always messing with me. I can't say or do anything without him mocking me, calling me names, or making fun of me when I raise my hand or try to read out loud in class. He always does it when no one is looking, and the teacher never catches him. It really hurts my feelings. The other day at lunch, he stole my sandwich and told me not to tell on him or else he would beat me up after school. I went hungry. At recess, he steals the basketballs so I can't play, and he tells everyone not to pick me for their team because I am a loser. I'm starting to think maybe I am a loser. Other people are nice to me, but only when this kid is not around. I just can't take it anymore. What should I do?

Signed,

Sad in School

Letter 3

Dear School Editor,

I think I might have a problem. You see, I want to be liked, **more liked** than anyone else. I get jealous when I see my friends talking to others, and sometimes I tell them they can't be friends with me or come to my birthday party if they are nice to other kids that I don't really like. There's a new girl at our school that I really can't stand. She's pretty and a really great volleyball player, and I've made up a few rumors about her to get people to ignore her at lunch and not let her sit with them. It's a game to me sometimes, to see what I can get others to do just to keep me as their friend. Maybe I'm jealous or just want to be the center of attention. What should I do?

Signed,

Controlling the Classroom

Follow-up: What advice did you give to the writers of these letters that you could apply to yourself in similar situations?

LESSON 10
CONFLICT

We all have conflict in our lives from time to time, whether it is an argument with a brother or sister or a disagreement with your best friend. Experiencing conflict is difficult. It can make you feel frustrated, angry, disappointed, and even frightened.

In normal conflicts, both sides are able to work together to resolve the issue. Bullying is not a normal conflict. Intimidation is usually involved, and the person who is bullying usually does not recognizing there is a problem and does not appreciate the impact of their behavior on others.

No matter how much you work to bully-proof yourself, learning to express yourself when you *are* dealing with difficult situations is extremely important.

ACTIVITY

Color the rectangle below to represent what conflict looks and feels like to you. Be prepared to discuss why you made your choices and what each color represents to you.

Describe your color choices and what they mean to you:

_____
_____
_____
_____
_____
_____
_____

ACTIVITY

Answer the following questions about conflict and how you deal with situations.

Select Never, Sometimes, Usually, or Always for each question:

	Never	Sometimes	Usually	Always
I am kind to others, even when an adult is not looking.	☐	☐	☐	☐
Other kids often get into conflict with each other.	☐	☐	☐	☐
I often get into conflict with others.	☐	☐	☐	☐
I wish I knew how to handle conflict better.	☐	☐	☐	☐
I bully others.	☐	☐	☐	☐
I get bullied by others.	☐	☐	☐	☐
I know how to manage my anger.	☐	☐	☐	☐
Other kids manage their anger well.	☐	☐	☐	☐
I feel safe around other kids.	☐	☐	☐	☐
I feel unsafe and scared around other kids.	☐	☐	☐	☐

Tell about a conflict you were involved in. Describe what happened. How did it end? Was it solved?

_____
_____
_____
_____
_____
_____
_____

What did you learn about yourself from this experience and conflict with others?

_____
_____
_____
_____
_____
_____
_____

LESSON 11
MISSION: BULLY-PROOFING MYSELF

Bullying happens sometimes, but that doesn't mean you can't help bully-proof yourself. What does that mean? Bully-proofing yourself means building your skills, courage, and confidence to handle bullying if it happens. It also helps you send the message to others that you are not an easy target.

KEYS TO BULLY-PROOFING YOURSELF

- **Talk to an adult you trust:** Agree on a plan of action if you are bullied or witness someone else being bullied. This way you know that you have support and have an idea of how to handle a situation if you are faced with it.

- **Don't believe a word they say:** "Sticks and stones may break my bones, but words will never hurt me" is a popular saying that isn't necessarily true. Words can and do hurt, but if you know that nothing bullies say about you is true and it's more about their state of mind, it's easier to ignore them and not believe what they are saying to you. No matter what they say, you are a valuable and strong person. Don't believe them.

- **Assert yourself:** Practice and remember some things you could say in return if someone is bullying you. Example: *I know that I'm not stupid. I want you to leave me alone.*

- **Stay calm:** Those who are bullying often pick on people they know will react emotionally. They feel more power and control because they caused that reaction. Instead, just remain calm. Ignore them. Walk away. Don't give them the satisfaction.

- **Basic avoidance:** Students who bully often strike when adults are not present. Avoid unsupervised areas like empty hallways, bathrooms away from the main hall, or certain areas of the playground that are out of the line of sight of a teacher or other adult.

- **Fake it:** Even if you aren't feeling brave and strong, act like you are. It is important that the person bullying you thinks that you are.

- **Build yourself up:** Know that you are important, you are cared for, and you matter!

- **Use imagery:** Imagine situations where you are assertive and the situation ends well.

ACTIVITY

Knowing how to bully-proof yourself is important, but you will still face challenges. Come up with a plan of action to help you navigate your way through those challenges. Post this list somewhere so that you can refer back to it anytime you need to!

1. An adult I can trust to talk to when faced with a bullying challenge:

    _____

2. If someone says something to me that I know is not true, I will:

    _____

    _____

3. Something I can say in return to a mean comment to be assertive and let others know that I am not an easy target is:

    _____

    _____

    _____

4. Ways to remain calm when faced by a bullying challenge are:

    _____

    _____

    _____

5. Ways to avoid being in a bullying situation are:

    _____

    _____

    _____

6. When I'm feeling weak and afraid inside but want to appear to be brave and strong on the outside, I will:

    _____

    _____

    _____

7. One thing I will tell myself every day to remind me that I am valuable and important is:

    _____

    _____

    _____

LESSON 12
BREATHE EASY

How many times have you felt stressed? Sometimes you feel like there is nothing you can do, but taking a few deep breaths can really change your mood, reduce your stress level, and even make you healthier!

Breathing and taking deep breaths are very different. There are many benefits to learning how to take deep breaths:

1. You'll sleep better.

2. You'll be healthier.

3. You'll improve concentration in school.

4. You'll handle anxiety and stress better.

5. You'll be able to better problem-solve situations and overcome challenges.

6. You'll be able to remain calmer.

7. You will think more clearly.

Source: *http://www.babyzone.com/kids/kids-health-and-safety/teach-deep-breathing_66211*

ACTIVITY: LEARN TO TAKE DEEP BREATHS

If you have the space, lie on your back with a hand on your heart and another hand on your belly. Take a deep breath through your nose and watch as your belly rises. Try holding this breath for at least three seconds, and then slowly exhale. Deep breaths move your whole midsection, but shallow breaths only move your upper body. You can also do this exercise while seated or standing. You can take deep breaths anywhere!

Let's Practice

1. Inhale through your nose, expanding your belly, then fill your chest, counting to four.

2. Hold and count to four.

3. Exhale fully from slightly parted mouth, counting to four.

Taking deep breaths is a skill that you can easily learn that will help you in so many areas of your life. Deep breaths can help you calm down during stressful situations or help clear your mind before a big test. By making time to take 10 deep breaths, you will feel more calm and begin to think more clearly.

ACTIVITY: MAKING STRESS BALLS

Another way to release stress is to use a stress ball. This is something you can carry with you, keep in your pocket, or reach for when you are feeling nervous or experiencing stress. Squeeze it in your hand to release tension.

You can make your own stress ball with some easy-to-obtain materials:

- two 11-inch latex balloons, latex gloves, or vinyl gloves
- dried beans

Fill one balloon with beans and tie a knot. Cut off the top of the second balloon and stretch over the first balloon for added durability.

Reflection: Think of a time you were stressed. How do you think using breathing exercises or a stress ball might be able to help you deal with your feelings next time you are confronted with them?

_____
_____
_____
_____
_____
_____
_____
_____
_____

LESSON 13
WHO I AM

Reflecting on yourself is important and reminds us of our foundation. Answer the following questions. Fill in each blank with at least one answer.

_____ makes me happy.

_____ upsets me.

_____ makes me angry.

_____ scares me.

_____ makes me laugh.

_____ stresses me.

Something I need in my life _____

Something I really want to happen _____

The people in my life who are most important to me _____

My greatest wish for my future _____

ACTIVITY: THIS IS WHO I AM . . .

You will introduce yourself to a classmate, sharing your answers. As you share, ask yourself how you can show respect while listening. Give your classmate your full attention, and ask questions as they come up. When your partner finishes sharing his or her information, you will do three things:

1. Tell the person something new you learned about him or her.

2. Share with the person something that you both have in common.

3. Compliment the person on something he or she shared with you today.

Journal reflection: What did you learn about your partner from this activity? What did you learn about yourself?

_____
_____
_____
_____
_____

LESSON 14
POSITIVE SELF-TALK

"No one can make you feel inferior without your consent." —Eleanor Roosevelt

What do you think Eleanor Roosevelt meant when she said this? Do you agree? Why or why not? Explain.

_____
_____
_____

When you accept yourself, you know that you are valuable as a person. When you recognize your value, it does not matter what others say about you. What others say does not change what you know to be true already.

Self-esteem is a positive feeling that you have about yourself. When you have good self-esteem, you can build your self-acceptance.

What is **self-acceptance**? It is the knowing that you have self-worth and value as a person regardless of any faults or weaknesses that you might have.

When you are used to hearing negative messages from others, it is easy to believe negative things about yourself. Positive self-talk is a great way to help you improve your self-acceptance. When you focus on your strengths and speak to yourself in a positive way, you remind yourself that you are a good and valuable person who is worthy.

Examples of Positive Self-Talk

I am important.   I will be a successful person, no matter how many mistakes I make.

ACTIVITY: FINISH THESE SENTENCES BELOW

I am a good friend. A time I was a good friend to someone was

_____
_____
_____

I am loved and others care about me. People who care about me are

_____
_____
_____

I am capable of achieving success. A time when I felt successful was

_____
_____
_____
_____

I am talented. Some things that I am good at are

_____
_____
_____
_____

I am able to make good decisions. A time I made a really good decision was

_____
_____
_____
_____

Practice saying positive things about yourself! What other positive self-talk can you add here?

_____
_____
_____
_____

ACTIVITY: CREATE YOUR OWN POSITIVE SELF-TALK MOTTO

When you speak to yourself positively, you will think more positively about yourself.

Create your own positive self-talk motto that you will repeat daily and use to build self-acceptance.

Sample: *I am* special. *I can* be anything I want to be. *I will* celebrate who I am each day.

I am _____.

I can _____.

I will _____.

Source: *Self-Talk: A Child's Bulletproof Vest Against Emotional Gunfire* by Devin C. Hughes

LESSON 15
STICKS AND STONES CAN BREAK MY BONES... AND WORDS CAN REALLY HURT ME!

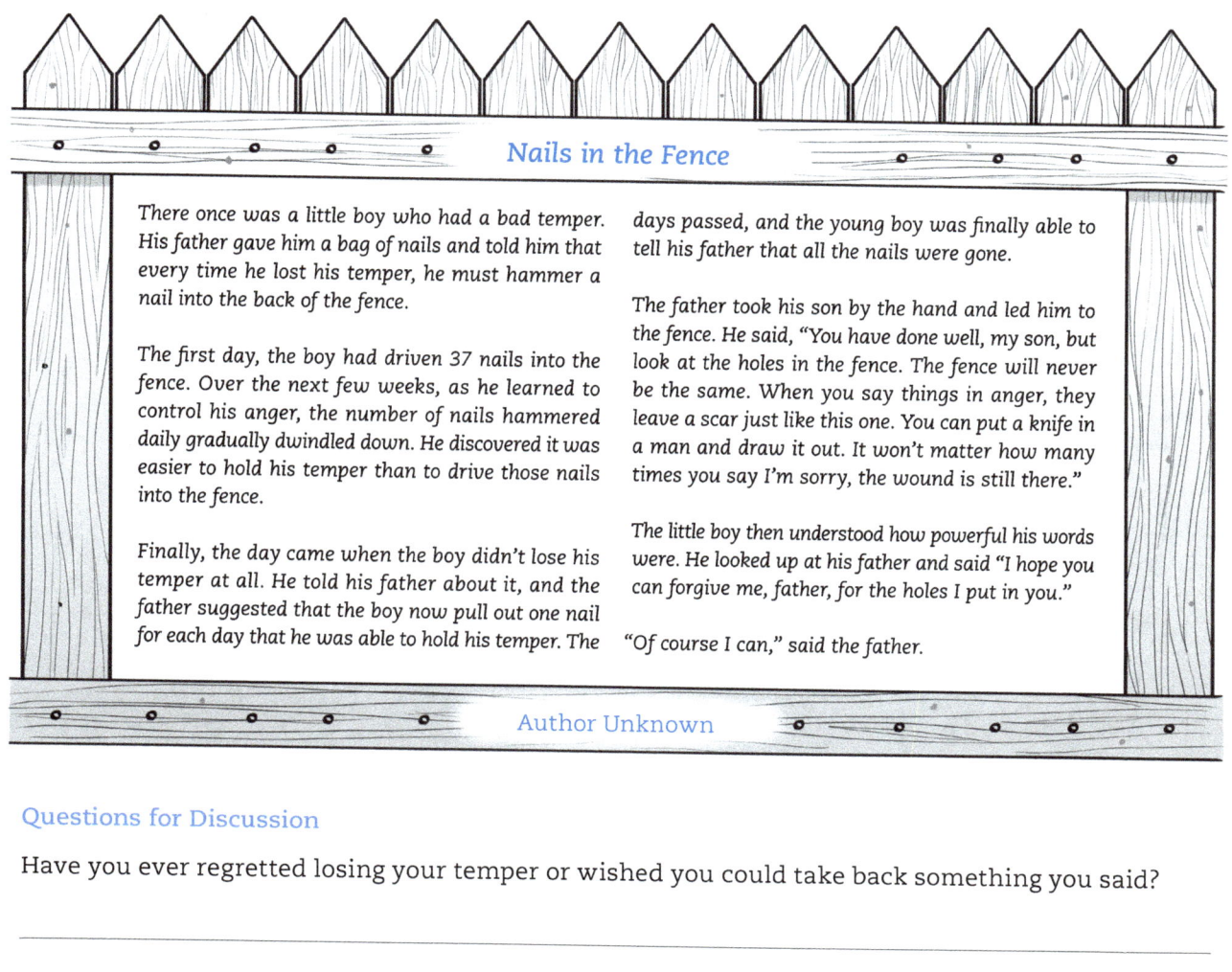

Nails in the Fence

There once was a little boy who had a bad temper. His father gave him a bag of nails and told him that every time he lost his temper, he must hammer a nail into the back of the fence.

The first day, the boy had driven 37 nails into the fence. Over the next few weeks, as he learned to control his anger, the number of nails hammered daily gradually dwindled down. He discovered it was easier to hold his temper than to drive those nails into the fence.

Finally, the day came when the boy didn't lose his temper at all. He told his father about it, and the father suggested that the boy now pull out one nail for each day that he was able to hold his temper. The days passed, and the young boy was finally able to tell his father that all the nails were gone.

The father took his son by the hand and led him to the fence. He said, "You have done well, my son, but look at the holes in the fence. The fence will never be the same. When you say things in anger, they leave a scar just like this one. You can put a knife in a man and draw it out. It won't matter how many times you say I'm sorry, the wound is still there."

The little boy then understood how powerful his words were. He looked up at his father and said "I hope you can forgive me, father, for the holes I put in you."

"Of course I can," said the father.

Author Unknown

Questions for Discussion

Have you ever regretted losing your temper or wished you could take back something you said?

Do you think that the father did the right thing in forgiving his son?

Is forgiveness an important lesson to learn, or is it just something you do?

ACTIVITY: SORRY IS A START

In lesson 3, you wrote a letter about a time when you might have bullied someone or witnessed someone who was being bullied. Now that we have learned more about bullying, how to be a positive influence, and how to combat the negative comments that may be made to you or others, take some time to rewrite the letter. Is there anything you wish you could say now that you didn't before? Now is your chance.

Dear

I wanted to write you a letter to tell you that I am sorry.*

At the time, I acted the way I did because

When it happened, I thought and felt

You may have thought and felt

Now, as I think back

I know I cannot take back what happened, but I wanted to let you know that I am sorry and in the future I will

Sincerely,

*Explain your reasons for being sorry, whether it is something you did or something you did not do and should have.

Time to reflect: Scars are reminders of an accident or injury we experienced. They tell a story and usually scars can be seen by others. Scars that are caused by bullying and hurt can't always be seen by others, but the pain and hurt often remains. What do you think about this? What are some ways you could try to take away the pain others might feel from the scars of bullying they carry with them? How can you help others who feel guilty about the scars they have caused others?

LESSON 16
BE AN UPSTANDER

We've discussed what a bystander is, but what is an upstander? An **upstander** is a person who bravely makes the choice to do the right thing: To stand up for someone who needs support, encouragement, and help.

When you choose to be an upstander, you are making it publicly known that the bullying behavior you are seeing is not acceptable. Being an upstander means supporting someone else in a kind and compassionate way, recognizing that everyone involved has feelings and concerns. Being an upstander takes courage because it is hard to do sometimes, but it is the right thing to do.

In the diagram below, write some of the similarities and differences between the bystander and the upstander. What do they have in common? What makes them different?

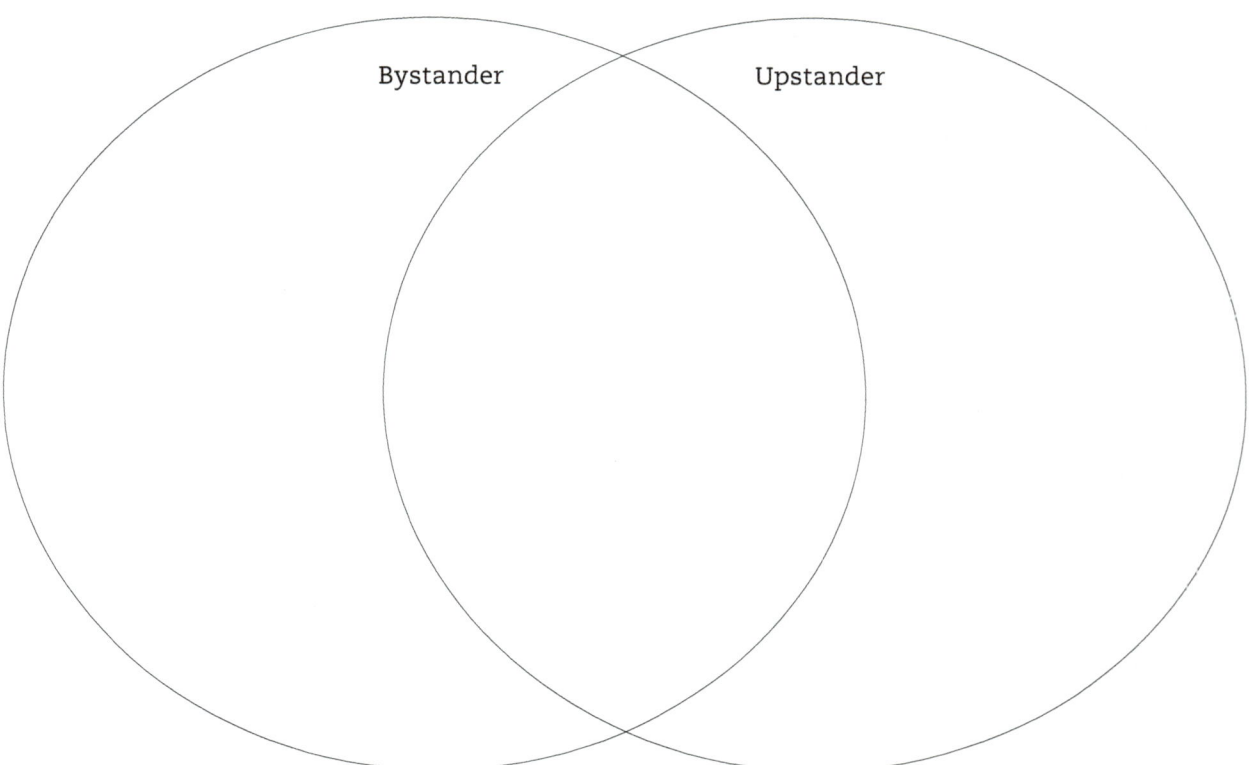

"I am only one; but still I am one. I cannot do everything, but still I can do something. I will not refuse to do the something I can do." —Helen Keller

What do you think Helen Keller meant by her quote above? How does this relate to being an upstander?

_____
_____
_____
_____

ACTIVITY: PUT YOUR COURAGE ON DISPLAY

Bumper stickers are a great way to display something you believe in. Some cars are filled with bumper stickers that tell you a lot about the person who drives that car. Today, you are going to design a bumper sticker that represents your commitment to being an upstander. It can be a thought, a quote, or a reminder to others and can include drawings or just words. Whatever you choose to put on your bumper sticker, remember that it represents your courage and beliefs about your responsibility to do the right thing.

Examples:

TAKE A STAND. LEND A HAND.

Niceness is *priceless*.

Explain your bumper sticker here. What message do you hope it sends to others about you?

_____
_____
_____
_____
_____
_____
_____
_____
_____
_____

LESSON 17
SHOWING COMPASSION & UNDERSTANDING FOR THE BULLY, TOO

Sometimes those who hurt us and hurt others need our understanding and forgiveness the most. In fact, people who bully are often the victim themselves. People who are bullying may be craving attention, support, care, and understanding, even though they might not be able to accurately communicate those needs.

Extending love and kindness to **everyone**, even those who are most undeserving in the moment, can actually make a big difference. It's hard to hate someone who is showing kindness. Isn't it time to break the cycle? Could you respond with compassion and care instead?

> "People must learn to hate, and if they can learn to hate, they can be taught to love, for love comes more naturally to the human heart than its opposite." —Nelson Mandela

ACTIVITY: RESPONDING WITH COMPASSION

Next time you hear a negative comment said to you or someone else, how could you respond with compassion and care to the person spreading that negativity? Practice with the chart below:

Bullying Comment	Responding with Compassion and Care
No one likes you. You have no friends.	I do have friends. And I'd like to be friends with you, too.
You are so stupid!	_____
School would be better without you.	_____
You aren't good at doing anything!	_____
Nice outfit, dork.	_____
You can't sit with us.	_____

Everyone matters and everyone deserves to be understood. Showing compassion and kindness to someone who hurts you and others takes courage, but it also builds your character.

ACTIVITY: FEEDING THE WOLF

Read the story below and answer the discussion questions.

An old Cherokee Indian told his grandson, "My son, there is a battle between two wolves inside all of us.

One is Evil. It is anger, jealousy, greed, resentment, inferiority, lies, and ego. The other is Good. It is joy, peace, love, hope, humility, kindness, empathy, and truth."

The boy thought about it and asked, "Grandfather, which wolf wins?"

The old man quietly replied, "The one you feed."

—Author Unknown

Questions for Discussion

We each have two "wolves" inside of us. We feed our wolves daily based on our thoughts and the choices we make with our thoughts. Do you think this is true? Why or why not?

_____

_____

Do you think that others help feed our "wolves" both negatively and positively? Explain.

_____

_____

In what ways can you choose to be a pack leader and nurture the good inside of you and others?

_____

_____

LESSON 18
THE COMMUNITY CHALLENGE

Your community is made up of different kinds of people. It is those differences that make the world a more interesting place. Celebrating differences and accepting that everyone has a purpose, a right to be who they are, and a right to feel safe is part of your responsibility as a member of your community.

ACTIVITY

Match the following words to their definitions:

1. Included   a. Sympathetic concern for the sufferings or misfortunes of others

2. Valued   b. Considered to be important, cherished

3. Accepted   c. Contained within a part of a whole, considered

4. Respectful   d. Recognized as valid or correct

5. Compassion   e. Showing deep admiration for someone or something

ACTIVITY

Building up your community is a big responsibility. Brainstorm some ways you can carry out the challenge of being a valuable member of your community below.

I can help others feel included in my community by:

_____

_____

_____

I can make others in my community feel valued by:

_____

_____

_____

I can show others acceptance in my community by:

_____

_____

_____

I can be respectful of others in my community by:

_____

_____

_____

I can demonstrate compassion for others in my community by:

_____

_____

_____

Do you accept the Community Challenge? If so, sign your name below.

I believe that everybody has the right to live in a community where they feel safe, included, valued, and accepted, regardless of any differences. I pledge to be respectful of others and stand up against bullying whenever and wherever I see it, and show compassion to all.

_____   _____
Your Signature   Date

LESSON 19
WE CAN ALL BE HEROES

We all have the power to stop bullying. We all have the power to change a person's life by doing the right thing. We all have the power to choose to be kind and help everyone respect each other. We can all be heroes.

What is a hero? A person who is admired or idealized for courage, outstanding achievements, or noble qualities.

List some heroes that you know of here. They can be famous or not. All that matters is that you admire them for some reason.

Heroes

In what ways can you be a hero to others?

1. _____
2. _____
3. _____

ACTIVITY: ACROSTIC POEM

You are going to write an acrostic poem. An acrostic poem uses the letters from a word to create lines of poetry about the subject. These lines do not have to rhyme, but they do have to relate to the topic. Start each line of the poem with the letters below.

Sample:

> Playing around with words
> Open your mind to ideas
> Each word adds to the story
> My poem is now complete!

Your Topic: HEROES

H _____

E _____

R _____

O _____

E _____

S _____

> "Hard times don't create heroes. It is during the hard times when the 'hero' within us is revealed." —Bob Riley

LESSON 20
WE ARE HOW WE TREAT EACH OTHER AND NOTHING MORE

Nothing More
by The Alternate Routes

To be humble, to be kind.
It is the giving of the peace in your mind.
To a stranger, To a friend
To give in such a way that has no end.

We are Love
We are One
We are how we treat each other when the day is done.
We are Peace
We are War
We are how we treat each other and Nothing More

To be bold, to be brave.
It is the thinking that the heart can still be saved
And the darkness can come quick
The Dangers in the Anger and the hanging on to it.

We are Love
We are One
We are how we treat each other when the day is done.
We are Peace
We are War
We are how we treat each other and Nothing More

Tell me what it is that you see
A world that's filled with endless possibilities?
**Heroes don't look like they used to,
they look like you do.**

We are Love
We are One
We are how we treat each other when the day is done.
We are Peace
We are War
We are how we treat each other and Nothing More

Permission to print and use lyrics granted by the Alternate Routes; http://www.alternateroutes.com.

Reflection: Read the lyrics of the song "Nothing More" on the left. What do the words tell you about bullying and how we treat each other? What is one thing you have learned?

_____
_____
_____
_____
_____
_____
_____
_____
_____
_____
_____
_____
_____
_____
_____
_____
_____
_____
_____
_____
_____
_____
_____
_____
_____

RESOURCES

Anderson, Connie, Ph.D. "IAN Research Report: Bullying and Children with ASD." Interactive Autism Network. *http://www.iancommunity.org/cs/ianresearch_reports/ian_research_report_bullying.*

Anthes, Emily. "Inside the Bullied Brain." *The Boston Globe*, November 28, 2010, *http://www.boston.com/bostonglobe/ideas/articles/2010/11/28/inside_the_bullied_brain.*

Dominguez, John. "Tackling Peer Harassment." *Quintessential Barrington*, Sept–Oct. 2012, 48.

Fields, R. Douglas. "The New Brain," *Psychology Today*, October 30, 2010, *http://www.psychologytoday.com/blog/the-new-brain/201010/sticks-and-stones-hurtful-words-damage-the-brain.*

Massachusetts Advocates for Children. "Targeted, Taunted, Tormented: The Bullying of Children with Autism Spectrum Disorder." *http://www.massadvocates.org/documents/Bullying-Report_000.pdf.*

Melloy, Kilian. "Your Brain on Bullying." *Edge Boston*, March 21, 2011, *http://www.edgeboston.com/columnists/kilian_melloy///117045/your_brain_on_bullying.*

PACER's National Bullying Prevention Center. "Peer Advocacy." *http://www.pacer.org/bullying/resources/students-with-disabilities/peer-advocacy.asp.*

StopBullying.gov. "Bullying Statistics in America." *http://www.nobullying.com/bullying-statistics.*

StopBullying.gov. "What is Bullying." *http://www.stopbullying.gov/what-is-bullying/definition/index.html.*

University of Rochester Medical Center. "Children With Both Autism And ADHD Often Bully, Parents Say: Researchers Caution Against Labeling." *ScienceDaily*, May 18, 2007. *http://www.sciencedaily.com/releases/2007/05/070517100417.htm.*

Walsh, David. "The Bullied Brain." *Huffington Post*, August 1, 2011, *http://www.huffingtonpost.com/david-walsh/the-bullied-brain_b_914709.html, 8/1/11.*

"About the Bully Project," The Bully Project, accessed July 29, 2013, *http://www.thebullyproject.com/about_the_bully_project.*

KRISTIN WESTBERG

BIOGRAPHY

With nine years of middle school teaching experience as well as an M.S. in Youth Development Leadership and a M.Ed. in Higher Ed Administration, **Kristin Westberg** thoroughly understands the practice and theory of creating an environment that is intolerant of bullying. As part of her role as RTC's director of operations, Kristin designs curriculum and creates workbooks and other teaching tools. Her work with *Those Who Bully and Those Who Are Bullied* is a culmination of her varied expertise.

As her own children progress through school, Kristin tries to instill the lessons in this workbook in them, in hopes that they will be "upstanders"—unwilling to ignore, encourage, or tolerate bullying.

ABOUT ORP

Oconomowoc Residential Programs, Inc. is an employee-owned family of companies whose mission is to make a difference in the lives of people with disabilities. Our dedicated staff of 2,000 employee owners provides quality services and professional care to more than 1,700 children, adolescents, and adults with special needs. ORP provides a continuum of care, including residential therapeutic education, community-based residential services, support services, respite care, treatment programs, and day services. The individuals in our care include people with developmental disabilities, physical disabilities, and intellectual disabilities. **Our guiding principle is passion:** a passion for the people we serve and for the work we do. For a comprehensive look at our programs and people, please visit *www.orp.com*.

ORP offers residential therapeutic education programs and alternative day schools among its array of services. These programs offer developmentally appropriate education and treatment for children, adolescents, and young adults in settings specially attuned to their needs. We provide special programs for students with specific academic and social issues relative to a wide range of disabilities, including autistic disorder, Asperger's disorder, mental retardation, anxiety disorders, depression, bipolar disorder, reactive attachment disorder, attention deficit disorder, Prader-Willi Syndrome, and other disabilities.

Genesee Lake School is a nationally recognized provider of comprehensive residential treatment, educational, and vocational services for children, adolescents, and young adults with emotional, mental health, neurological, or developmental disabilities. GLS has specific expertise in Autism Spectrum Disorders, anxiety and mood disorders, and behavioral disorders. We provide an individualized, person-centered, integrated team approach, which emphasizes positive behavioral support, therapeutic relationships, and developmentally appropriate practices. Our goal is to assist each individual to acquire skills to live, learn, and succeed in a community-based, less restrictive environment. GLS is particularly known for its high quality educational services for residential and day school students.

Genesee Lake School / Admissions Director
36100 Genesee Lake Road
Oconomowoc, WI 53066
262-569-5510
http://www.geneseelakeschool.com

T.C. Harris School is located in an attractive setting in Lafayette, Indiana. T.C. Harris teaches skills to last a lifetime, through a full therapeutic program as well as day school and other services.

T.C. Harris School / Admissions Director
3700 Rome Drive
Lafayette, IN 47905
765-448-4220
http://www.tcharris.com

T.C. Harris Academy is a private school option, in the local community, that works not only to stabilize a student's behavior in a therapeutic setting, but also help them thrive academically. Our goal is simple: provide students with the skills they need to function effectively and achieve greater success.

T.C. Harris Academy
3746 Rome Drive
Lafayette, IN 47905
765-448-9989
http://www.tcharris.com

Transitions Academy provides behavioral health and educational services to adolescents in a 24-hour structured residential setting. Treatment services are offered that are best practice and evidence based, targeting social, emotional, behavioral, and mental health impairments. Transitions Academy serves children from throughout the United States.

Transitions Academy / Admissions Director
11075 North Pennsylvania Street
Indianapolis, IN 46280
Toll Free: 1-844-488-0448
admissions@transitions-academy.com

The Richardson School is a day school in West Allis, Wisconsin that provides an effective, positive alternative education environment serving children from Milwaukee, Beloit, and their surrounding communities.

The Richardson School / Director
6753 West Roger Street
West Allis, WI 53219
414-540-8500
http://www.richardsonschool.com

THE ORP LIBRARY

BULLYING

CLASSROOM HEROES
ONE CHILD'S STRUGGLE WITH BULLYING AND A TEACHER'S MISSION TO CHANGE SCHOOL CULTURE

HOW TO BE A HERO
A COMIC BOOK ABOUT BULLYING

Nearly one third of all school children face physical, verbal, cyber, or social bullying on a regular basis. Educators and parents search for ways to end bullying, but as that behavior becomes more sophisticated, it's harder to recognize and stop. In *Classroom Heroes*, Jason is a quiet, socially awkward seventh grader who has long suffered bullying in silence. His parents notice him becoming angrier and more withdrawn, but they don't realize the scope of the problem until one bully takes it too far—and one teacher acts on her determination to stop it. Both *Classroom Heroes* and *How to Be a Hero*—along with a supporting coloring book (*Heroes in the Classroom*) and curriculum guide (*Those Who Bully and Those Who Are Bullied*)—recognize that stopping bullying requires a change in mindset: adults and children must create a community that simply does not tolerate bullying. These books provide practical yet very effective strategies to end bullying, one student at a time.

ASPERGER'S DISORDER

MELTDOWN

ASPERGER'S DISORDER, CHALLENGING BEHAVIOR, AND A FAMILY'S JOURNEY TOWARD HOPE

MELTING DOWN

A COMIC FOR KIDS WITH ASPERGER'S DISORDER AND CHALLENGING BEHAVIOR

Meltdown and its companion comic book, *Melting Down*, are both based on the fictional story of Benjamin, a boy diagnosed with Asperger's disorder and additional challenging behavior. From the time Benjamin is a toddler, he and his parents know he is different: he doesn't play with his sister, refuses to make eye contact, and doesn't communicate well with others. And his tantrums are not like normal tantrums; they're meltdowns that will eventually make regular schooling—and day-to-day life—impossible. Both the prose book, intended for parents, educators, and mental health professionals, and the comic for the kids themselves demonstrate that the journey toward hope isn't simple . . . but with the right tools and teammates, it's possible.

THE ORP LIBRARY

AUTISM SPECTRUM DISORDER

MR. INCREDIBLE
A STORY ABOUT AUTISM, OVERCOMING CHALLENGING BEHAVIOR, AND A FAMILY'S FIGHT FOR SPECIAL EDUCATION RIGHTS

INCREDIBLE ADAM AND A DAY WITH AUTISM
AN ILLUSTRATED STORY INSPIRED BY SOCIAL NARRATIVES

Mr. Incredible shares the fictional story of Adam, a boy diagnosed with autistic disorder. On Adam's first birthday, his mother recognizes that something is different about him: he recoils from the touch of his family, preferring to accept physical contact only in the cool water of the family's pool. As Adam grows older, he avoids eye contact, is largely nonverbal, and has very specific ways of getting through the day; when those habits are disrupted, intense meltdowns and self-harmful behavior follow. From seeking a diagnosis to advocating for special education services, from keeping Adam safe to discovering his strengths, his family becomes his biggest champion. The journey to realizing Adam's potential isn't easy, but with hope, love, and the right tools and teammates, they find that Adam truly is *Mr. Incredible*. The companion comic in this series, inspired by social stories, offers an innovative, dynamic way to guide children—and parents, educators, and caregivers—through some of the daily struggles experienced by those with autism.

FAMILY SUPPORT

CHASING HOPE
YOUR COMPASS FOR A NEW NORMAL
NAVIGATING THE WORLD OF THE SPECIAL NEEDS CHILD

Schuyler Walker was just four years old when he was diagnosed with autism, bipolar disorder, and ADHD. In 2004, childhood mental illness was rarely talked about or understood. With knowledge and resources scarce, Schuyler's mom, Christine, navigated a lonely maze to determine what treatments, medications, and therapies could benefit her son. In the ten years since his diagnosis, Christine has often wished she had a "how to" guide that would provide the real mom-to-mom information she needed to survive the day and, in the end, help her family navigate the maze with knowledge, humor, grace, and love. Christine may not have had a manual at the beginning of her journey, but she hopes this book will serve as yours.

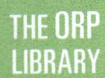

PRADER-WILLI SYNDROME

INSATIABLE
A PRADER-WILL STORY

ULTRA-VIOLET
ONE GIRL'S
PRADER-WILLI STORY

Estimated to occur once in every 15,000 births, Prader-Willi Syndrome is a rare genetic disorder that includes features of cognitive disabilities, problem behaviors, and, most pervasively, chronic hunger that leads to dangerous overeating and its life-threatening consequences. *Insatiable: A Prader-Willi Story* and its companion comic book, *Ultra-Violet: One Girl's Prader-Willi Story*, draw on dozens of intensive interviews to offer insight into the world of those struggling with Prader-Willi Syndrome. Both books tell the fictional story of Violet, a vivacious young girl born with the disorder, and her family, who—with the help of experts—will not give up their quest to give her a healthy and happy life.

REACTIVE ATTACHMENT DISORDER

AN UNLIKELY TRUST
ALINA'S STORY OF ADOPTION, COMPLEX TRAUMA, HEALING, AND HOPE

ALINA'S STORY
LEARNING HOW TO TRUST, HEAL, AND HOPE

An Unlikely Trust: Alina's Story of Adoption, Complex Trauma, Healing, and Hope, and its companion children's book, *Alina's Story*, share the journey of Alina, a young girl adopted from Russia. After living in an orphanage during her early life, Alina is unequipped to cope with the complexities of the outside world. She has a deep mistrust of others and finds it difficult to talk about her feelings. When she is frightened, overwhelmed, or confused, she lashes out in rages that scare her family. Alina's parents know she needs help and work endlessly to find it for her, eventually discovering a special school that will teach Alina new skills. Slowly, Alina gets better at expressing her feelings and solving problems. For the first time in her life, she realizes she is truly safe and loved . . . and capable of loving in return.

Also look for books on children and psychotropic medications coming soon!

www.ingramcontent.com/pod-product-compliance
Lightning Source LLC
LaVergne TN
LVHW081400060426
835510LV00016B/1915